THE POWER OF SELF-CONFIDENCE

9 steps to boost your self-esteem, conquer your fears and learn to love yourself

Daniel J. Martin

Disclaimer: This book has been created with the intention of providing information, suggestions, and guidance on various areas of life, including emotional well-being, mental health, personal growth, and the development of healthy relationships. However, it does not substitute for professional medical care or the advice of a qualified psychologist or therapist. If you are facing serious mental or emotional health issues, we recommend you seek professional help immediately.

In the end, we only regret the chances we didn't take.

CONTENTS

DOWNLOAD THE AUDIOBOOK FREE!

*If you would rather enjoy **The power of self-confidence** on the go, **you can download its audio version completely FREE!***

www.danieljmartin.es/audio/psc

Introduction

We all want a life full of success, happiness and fullness. Sadly, most people will never experience these emotions in a sustained way or to the extent that they want for most of their lives. For many, life feels like stumbling from failure to failure, from one setback to another, from one loss to the next. Their existence becomes drained and they lose interest in life.

But why?

Usually, a lack of confidence is the main issue. It's not external factors that make success difficult; it's the fact that many people don't trust their own abilities. This means they spend too much time worrying they're not good enough, rather than concentrating on their strong points.

How important is self-confidence?

Self-confidence is the most significant difference between the «average human» and people like Elon Musk, Richard Branson, Steve Jobs and Jeff Bezos, to name but a few. People who reap higher levels of success are those who have greater confidence in their abilities and skills. They understand that despite the likelihood of obstacles along the way, trusting in their abilities will stop them from being knocked down. And, since they cannot be knocked down, success is just a matter of time. This is what enabled Thomas Edison to keep trying even after failing to invent the lightbulb over a thousand times. Self-confidence is what helped people like Nelson Mandela and Abraham Lincoln to change the course of history. It makes a difference!

Are you constantly battling low self-esteem? Do you have confidence issues? Do you consider yourself inferior to people around you? Do you question your actions because you think you're not good enough? Does negative criticism badly affect you? Do you find it hard to ask for what you want? Do you find yourself immersed in toxic relationships that bring you nothing good? Would you like to find out how to increase your self-confidence?

If you answered «yes» to any of these questions, you're reading the right book. I also suffered with confidence problems in my teenage years. I would shy away from social gatherings because I didn't know how to act or behave. I downplayed my achievements and wins by comparing them with what others had achieved. I didn't feel comfortable with my body, and that was reflected in the way I talked, walked, and related to others.

Luckily, over time, **I found a way to improve my self-confidence by using nine simple techniques or steps**: the same ones I'm about to share with you in this book, and which transformed me completely. This, along with the fact that I knew exactly what I wanted, was what enabled me to start reaching my goals and my confidence levels shot sky-high. I decided to write this book to share those nine steps - that it took me so many years to figure out - with people who find themselves in the same situation and need a guide to increasing their self-confidence in order to live a full, happy life.

Confidence in yourself may be the most important factor when it comes to achieving true happiness, inner peace and satisfaction. Not even success can fill the void that low self-esteem generates in our minds. I know many «successful» people with self-confidence problems. They are constantly worried about what others think of them. This lack of confidence prevents them from achieving true satisfaction. Similarly, I know «unsuccessful» people who have so much confidence in themselves that they enjoy full lives, with nothing to hold them back from achieving their destinies.

So... are you ready to begin your journey toward incredible self-esteem and confidence?

You only need to pack two things for this journey: knowledge, and action. I can take care of providing you with the **knowledge**. This book will be your guide. The techniques I'm going to explain are easy to apply and maintain. They are also proven to work - millions of people have used them, with surprising results. There's no doubt that they will work for you, too. However, you are the one who has to spring into **action** to turn the techniques into habits with the power to give you the life you've always dreamed of. In the words of Pablo Picasso: «Action is the foundational key to all success.»

The secret to self-confidence is knowing exactly what you want, and acting in a way that gets you closer to where you want to be.

Good luck!

Understanding self-confidence

«Love yourself first and everything else falls into line.»

— Lucille Ball

The Dalai Lama claims that anyone can change the world if they believe in their potential and have enough confidence in themselves. I completely agree, and I think self-confidence might even play a bigger role than potential. Confidence may just be the most important trait that determines our success or failure - especially in today's society.

Many talented people never achieve success - there are countless examples of this. You've probably heard stories of geniuses hindered by their lack of confidence. Often, the difference between two sportspeople of comparable talent boils down to their confidence levels. That's why you hear about successful athletes with a «winning mindset». A winning mindset is nothing more than confidence of the highest level.

A lack of confidence will stop you from reaching your full potential. Confidence is the result of your life experiences, which condition your mind to a certain way of thinking and of viewing life. People with low self-confidence have too many negative thoughts. Their fear of failure stops them from living fully and from taking advantage of the opportunities life offers.

Most people have some degree of confidence problem, whether it's low self-esteem or confidence in excess. It comes as no surprise that low confidence is one of society's most common problems. We get so involved in other people's lives and business that external opinions end up depleting our self-esteem. Low self-esteem can also develop in childhood as a result of poor education or toxic parenting. That's why we have to take care of it at all times and all ages.

Everyone experiences low confidence at some point in their life. It becomes a real problem when people have low self-confidence permanently: people whose lack of confidence has become part of them. These people tend to be timid, submissive and passive. They hesitate whenever it's time to take any kind of action towards their dreams, and life passes them by. This irrational fear is caused by underestimating yourself, or overestimating the challenge ahead.

On the flip side of confidence problems is arrogance: the overestimation of one's own abilities and the underestimation of challenges faced.

Self-confidence is born of knowing yourself. It means being sure about your skills and abilities to take on the challenges life throws your way.

Understanding that your actions will generate reward, and that this may be favorable or not, will help you overcome your fear of making mistakes, failing or being criticized in the course of going after what you want. However, confidence must be backed up by self-improvement. In fact, you can define self-confidence as the balance between knowing yourself and improving yourself. The only way to gain confidence is to take on challenges and keep improving your skills.

Boosting your self-confidence will improve your personal and professional life and help you mentally and physically as well as in your general relationships with the people around you.

Why you should develop greater self-confidence

Self-confidence gives you the courage you need to pursue the things you want. It's that feeling of believing in yourself that enables you to reach your greatest goals. It's the ability to turn your life around.

1. It makes you more assertive.

Confidence enables you to set appropriate, timely boundaries. You'll stop letting people push you about and you'll be able to say «no» without hesitation. A confident person knows how to defend themselves without intimidating others. Confidence will help you decide what you want and give you the assertiveness you need to go get it.

2. It helps you take control of your life.

People with low self-confidence tend to live according to what others want. They are incapable of making the decisions life asks of them. Confidence will teach you to stop dancing to other people's rhythm. You'll get better at making decisions and you'll be able to do what makes you happy, making things happen at the right time and in your own way.

3. It reduces your fear of criticism and rejection.

You will be able to walk straight up to the person you like, a prospective client or your boss to ask for the position you want. Confidence will enable you to put yourself out there without fear and without worrying what people will think, say, or do. Fear of rejection coupled with low self-esteem can stop you from acting. When you improve your confidence, you'll overcome that irrational fear.

4. It makes you braver and more resilient.

Confidence will push you to test your limits and dream big. It will enable you to fight for the desires of your heart despite failure and obstacles. You will be better at managing pressure and you won't be afraid to start over. And most important of all, the fear of making mistakes will no longer stand in your way.

5. It makes life better.

Life will take on more meaning and become more interesting and rewarding. Your life's purpose will be easier to understand and pursue. Confidence will make you more compassionate and empathetic toward other people, so you'll be better placed to make an impact on the lives of those around you.

6. It makes you happier.

Confidence goes hand-in-hand with more positive thinking, which will quiet negative thoughts and make you a happier person in various aspects of your life. Your mind will be more at peace, which will make overcoming your fears easier as you will always be able to find the silver lining. A person who is sure of themselves is a happy person. On the flip side, show me a person battling low confidence and low self-esteem and I'll show you an unhappy individual.

7. It increases your chances of success.

Confidence will make your potential and skills more secure. It will increase your chances of getting into action and enable you to better assess your abilities and requirements when faced with a challenge. In turn, this improves your chances of success, since you'll be better prepared and more likely to grab hold of the opportunities that come your way.

8. It makes you more attractive.

We all feel attracted to people who are sure of themselves. Self-confidence is reflected in your body language and your ability to hold a conversation, which makes you more appealing to prospective employers and romantic or professional partners. We all like confident people, because we love feeling that someone has everything under control.

9. Boost your leadership skills.

You can't convince others to trust you and believe in your abilities if you don't. Confidence will increase your self-esteem, and this will spread to people under you, allowing you to make better decisions and keep your team motivated.

Chapter summary

It doesn't matter how much you tell yourself you have to do something or change something in your life - whatever it is, it will be all but impossible to achieve if you don't have the confidence you need to take on the task. Confidence starts within. Once you have it, things become much easier; you become a more assertive person, your leadership qualities improve, you appear more attractive and your motivation to pursue and accomplish your goals will become unstoppable.

Accept yourself

«Be who you are and say what you feel, because those who mind don't matter and those who matter don't mind.»

— Dr. Seuss

Accepting yourself is the first step towards self-confidence. But in order to embrace who you are, first you need to know who you are. You wouldn't hug a total stranger, would you? So first you need to understand who you truly are.

Most people would answer the question «Who are you?» with their name, or some other means of identification, such as their profession. And that's correct in that the point of this question is usually to find out someone's identity. But do our names, papers or job titles really tell someone who we are?

Answering the question of who we are really requires more than just telling someone our first and last names. And in any case, there is much more than just one answer to the question. This is because there are many factors that come together to contribute to making us who we are. Broadly speaking, these factors could be classified as genetic or environmental.

Genetic factors give rise to personality traits that we inherit, such as eye color, dimples, straight or curly hair, and so on. And we don't just inherit our parents' appearances, but their cognitive and mental qualities, too. Environmental factors, on the other hand, are acquired. These traits are almost never physical. A good example would be someone's cognitive orientation in line with where they grew up and how they were raised. What I mean is that «what» we are depends on a number of factors, which can be categorized into these two groups.

Figure out who you really are

Now that you know the factors that help make up what you are, you might think that the idea of discovering who you are is pointless. But the battle to find out who we really are is not an easy one to win based solely on these factors - for more people. As human beings, we face new challenges every day: working, studying, learning and unlearning, getting it right, getting it wrong, and so on. Experiencing these new situations so often actually helps us keep discovering ourselves. In other words, we are perpetually learning who we are. Most of the factors that affect who we are pertain to our surroundings, so our personalities are mostly based on our experiences and how we react to them.

Even when it comes to genetic factors, we are also constantly discovering ourselves. This is because we sometimes find inherited traits we didn't know we had until we face life situations that cause them to manifest. Most traits of this type are cognitive. For example, you might not find out you're very good at accounting, until you're exposed to a situation or environment that requires the use of such skills. This means your environment actually affects your genetic factors.

To discover who you truly are, you need to be more adventurous. Go out more, meet new people, take part in more activities... Those big experiences with the capacity to change your life only happen when you leave your comfort zone. Travel to that place you always wanted to visit, attend that event or date you were thinking about canceling, dare to go see that movie you've had your eye on alone... You don't know just how much these things - no matter how small they may seem - can give you a new outlook on your personality.

As I said, all these experiences, our genetic traits, and environmental factors make us who we are. However, there are many other elements we need to bear in mind that make us unique. Reflect on everything you like and don't like: food, places, music, movies, sports, games, art, fashion... Take note of all of it; it's the only way you can really get to know yourself.

Embrace what you are

We've seen that we never stop discovering who we are, but that doesn't invalidate what you've found out about yourself so far. Today, you have a personality derived from genetic and environmental factors that have affected your existence up until this moment. As such, you now have a formed personality that you must accept and love. Embrace your personality. The first step to building unshakeable confidence in yourself is a very important one, and it consists of something as simple as loving who you are.

What exactly does it mean to love who you are? There's no doubt that you will come across certain flaws in your personality: weaknesses that can hinder you at times. Basically, loving yourself involves loving those defects. Your flaws could be physical - like a big nose or being too skinny. They can also be more abstract, like not feeling as smart as your colleagues. It's easy to love the parts of yourself that are readily accepted and attractive to other people, like a pretty smile or outgoing personality. These qualities captivate people and make them feel drawn to you, so it's tempting to allow your personality to revolve around them - but what about the parts of yourself other people don't like so much?

Focusing on your strong points (your generally acceptable, attractive attributes) is a good thing and it can boost your confidence. But even if you focus on your strengths, you can't avoid your flaws coming out every now and again. Most people with low confidence and self-esteem feel down when their flaws are revealed. That's a tough knock to the self-confidence they had built up around their virtues, which makes them feel even worse and batters their confidence even more.

You can't keep doing that to yourself. Even if you try hard to improve on them - which is a great idea - you have to understand that your weaknesses are part of you. Some of your flaws are not even your fault; you can't do much, if anything, about your appearance or your cognitive ability. So why do you afford them so much importance? The best you can do is take steps to minimize their effect on you, and try not to let them turn into a source of negativity.

This said, when your flaws negatively affect people around you, you do need to make a change. A good example would be anger issues. Anger is not a defect you can just accept; it can cause physical and psychological damage to those around you. Don't accept it with the excuse that you're trying to love who you are. If you need to, don't hesitate to seek professional help.

Another way to accept who you are is to stop trying to be like someone else. Many people pretend to have a different personality (usually by imitating somebody they admire) in order to earn affection or respect from others. The impression you create with this simulated personality won't last, because you can only pretend for so long. And when it runs out, your self-confidence will plummet and you will feel even worse about yourself, and even less inclined and motivated to achieve your goals.

The best way to improve your confidence is by being yourself. Don't pretend to like things you don't, and don't take part in activities that don't interest you for the sole purpose of pleasing others. Don't pretend to be something you're not - all it will do is damage who you really are.

Accepting yourself also means being honest with yourself: knowing your limits, knowing what you can and can't do, and knowing what you like and don't like. Don't try to hide it. Don't apologize for who you are. As long as your personality doesn't negatively impact on other people, then it doesn't matter what people say. This will really help to foster your self-confidence and make you an extraordinary person.

Chapter summary

If you are going to take just one thing away from this book, let it be: «be yourself». The fundamental root of a lack of confidence is usually not feeling comfortable with what you are or what you represent. The solution? Be yourself. Find out what you like and who you are, and then learn to love yourself. Don't make the mistake of trying to be like someone else. Don't pretend to be something you're not. Instead, focus on gradual improvement - both of what you like about yourself and what you don't like - while stacking up victories on your journey of self-development.

In the words of Steve Jobs: «Your time is limited, so don't waste it living someone else's life.»

STEP 2

Face your fears

«Don't be afraid of your fears. They're not there to scare you. They're there to let you know that something is worth it.»

— C. JoyBell

There is no human without fear, because fear is part of what makes us human. So why do we talk about fearless people? Being brave doesn't mean not being afraid - it means mastering, conquering, and being bigger than your fear. Fear is simply a protective measure that tells us to get ready for something that is about to happen.

When we study our evolution, we realize that just a few millennia ago, we weren't the dominant species on Earth that we are today. We were simply prey; our ability to distinguish between more shades of green than of any other color proves that, since green is the predominant color of nature. This feature of our vision made it easier for us to detect the presence of predators hidden among trees or in grass. It also helped us to find food and decide what was edible or not. As natural evolution tells us, this ability was born of a necessity for survival - in other words, our fear of going extinct. So we need fear - it tells us when to run and when to stay and fight.

The problem with fear is that it can take its job of protecting us too far, to the point where we become irrational. At that point, everything seems risky and everything that is hidden or unknown looks like a threat. The unknown can scare you so much that you're unable to act when opportunity knocks. Worry takes over, and your confidence can dip. When this happens, fear can dominate, control and paralyze you - and it only gets stronger, until it's an untamable monster.

In this situation, it's impossible to develop self-confidence. Fear generates so much doubt that you stop believing in yourself. To resolve this, let me give you some tips.

Five simple strategies for facing your fears

1. Identify your fear.

Fear is built around expectations of negative results, and it manifests as a «what if...». Our two greatest fears are the fears of failure and of rejection. I could list more, but these are the two that do more damage than all the others put together. The fear of failure has deprived us of so many innovations and great ideas, while the fear of rejection has destroyed many relationships even before they begin. You need to identify your fear before you can conquer it.

The problem is that fear is good at hiding. That's why it's a waste of time to discuss the various types of fear. Instead, try to find a word or situation that describes your fear. It doesn't matter how strange this word or situation may be, as long as you can clearly identify it. This level of understanding is the first step in turning fear from a scourge into an indispensable tool for our development, which is what it should be.

2. Wish it with all your might.

Doing what you have to do is discharging a duty. Doing what you want to do is seizing an opportunity. We both know which you would choose to do if you had the chance. You get excited when you have an opportunity, and there is no contest between excitement and fear. The former will always win hands down. When something excites us, our bodies release dopamine: a neurotransmitter which is responsible for our wellbeing, our motivation for taking on new tasks and feeling rewarded when deciding to do something. As such, when we do what we want - what makes us excited and enthusiastic - we have more opportunities to conquer the fear that stops us from reaching our goals.

Does this mean that you should only do things you're excited about? Of course not. It means you can overcome fear by finding something exciting in the things you have to do. One positive aspect is enough. Luckily, there's always a silver lining. You'll learn more about this when we reach the chapter on positive thinking. For now, just know that positivity wins out over negativity. So if you wish for something hard enough and find something positive about it, you'll be a step closer to overcoming your fears.

3. Don't walk alone.

I'll never get tired of stressing the importance of counting on valuable people in your life: people who support your projects, celebrate your wins, motivate you, or are simply there when you need them. We all need a shoulder to cry on and a sympathetic ear to vent to. But remember - lots of people will try to sabotage you. Read the chapter on how to manage criticism carefully. It's good to have company along the way and to hear other people's insights into things, as long as you stay away from any negativity. Try to surround yourself with positive people only - ones who add value to your life, rather than take it away.

4. Love the unknown.

Fear is about being afraid of change, of the unknown, of the possibility of unfavorable results. But the unknown is the most exciting thing about being alive. If you get locked in a room for just a few hours, you'll get unbelievably bored. Imagine how prison inmates feel. None of us, as free and living beings, should be afraid of change.

I know you try to stay away from things that cause you discomfort or unease, but that shouldn't happen at the expense of missing out on some of the most extraordinary experiences life offers.

Think about the first time you fell in love. Remember the feeling of being totally invincible, yet vulnerable at the same time? Or the amazing feeling of knowing someone was protecting and caring for you with no apparent motive? You never would have experienced anything like that if you hadn't had the courage to open yourself up to another person. Rewards only come when we decide to act.

Maybe your inner voice tells you that love is overrated, or that falling for someone will inevitably lead to your heart getting broken. But you know what? Both love and heartbreak are inescapable parts of being human. I firmly believe that everyone should have their heart broken at least once in their lives. This doesn't necessarily have to come from a romantic relationship; sadness, heartache, and failure are words that strike fear into our hearts - but only for a while. You will get over them, and they'll make you a better version of yourself.

Get out there and take risks! Make space for the unknown. Pray that it brings you amazing experiences, but get ready to go through a few setbacks, too. Fall down and get up again. It's the only way to keep growing.

5. Act.

None of what you learn in this book will be of any use to you whatsoever if you don't take the necessary action to get you closer to your goals. I know that's the difficult part, but you will never get anywhere if you don't take the first step. Failure is not the worst thing that could happen to you, and let me tell you something: most of your idols - I would go so far as to say all of them - have failed on countless occasions. Failure is not the end; it's barely the beginning. It's just a step along the way, and a necessary one on the path to achieving your goals. The more you do something, the more self-confidence you acquire. Similarly, the more you run away from the unknown, the bigger your fear grows. Taking action is, in itself, a powerful way to generate self-confidence. You will get better and stronger with every attempt. Michael Jordan didn't hit a slam dunk every time, nor did he win every match he ever played in - but we still consider him to be the greatest player of all time.

I often tell people that confidence has more to do with the journey than with the destination. Confidence is the ability to accept that you may not know how to do something, but that you can learn and improve. Confidence is about accepting that you aren't perfect. But be careful! Accepting that doesn't mean you shouldn't try to better yourself. You should practice things so that you can excel yourself every day. Professionals call this a growth mindset.

Taking action in a smart way will increase your chances of success. It's as simple as being prepared, and starting with baby steps. Your wins will be small, but your confidence will grow as you stack these small wins up. For example, let's imagine you're going to deliver a speech in public. To start with, I would advise you never to get up on stage without having first prepared and written your speech. So, the first thing is to draft and redraft it until you are satisfied with the result. The next step is to practice your speech in front of the mirror, and then in front of your friends. This approach will help you to make gradual progress until it's D-day. I call this a smart plan, because success tends to be the accumulation of multiple wins, rather than one big victory. So, stop making excuses. Fear is an excellent opportunity to put your courage and your limits to the test.

Chapter summary

We're all human, and it's perfectly normal to be afraid. But you shouldn't let your fears control you - they will hinder your chances of success if you let them take over your life. Fear is not necessarily a bad thing, but it can become bad depending on how you let it affect you. You can overcome it by identifying what it is that you're afraid of, loving the unknown, surrounding yourself with the right people, wishing for it enough and taking the necessary action to get you closer to your goals.

STEP 3

Think positive; silence that little voice in your head

«The positive thinker sees the invisible, feels the intangible, and achieves the impossible.»
— Winston Churchill

What makes one person an optimist and another a pessimist? Why do some people see the glass as half-full and others see it as half-empty? That little voice in your head is the culprit. It influences your emotions, your attitude and your wellbeing.

That inner voice is formed via your relationships with other human beings. Among them are your family members and friends, of course, but figures of authority such as your parents, guardians and teachers are those who normally have the greatest influence. During your development into adulthood, you internalize these influences and they become a part of your personality.

Your inner voice acts as an inescapable toxic shadow over your conscience, an enemy who identifies and exploits your weaknesses, an internal critic who attacks your confidence, self-esteem, relationships, health and mood. With every attack, it grows stronger - every doubt and waver increases its power over you, eroding your self-worth and creating a pessimistic view of the world. The only way out is to adopt positive thinking. Fortunately, this is something you can learn.

Some people think - wrongly - that positive thinking means ignoring your conscience. But the only thing it means is being optimistic and seeing the good side of things. It's about doing the opposite of what most people do: seeing the bad in every situation. Why not try it? Optimistic people are the happiest and most satisfied. They have self-confidence, they know their goals and work to achieve them. I'm sure you'd like to have those traits too, right?

Life is hard enough without making things more difficult for ourselves. Imagine how simple life is for someone who sees an opportunity in every problem compared to someone who sees a problem in every opportunity. Is it so hard to find the silver lining to every situation or person? Tell that to your inner voice! It's what separates the optimists from the pessimists, and what sets happy, confident, assertive and motivated people apart from the rest.

Both positive and negative thinking affect your mind, for the better or worse respectively. Science has shown that the thoughts you feed your mind with affect your body, too. So, the consequences of your thoughts go beyond their mental effects and extend to your physical health. Optimistic people are more creative, live longer, have better resistance to illness, heal faster and have higher pain thresholds - all this and more, with zero side effects.

Nine simple tips to help you think positive

Making the most of the power of positive thinking is simple in theory, but it takes a lot of strength and discipline. If you can manage it, anything is possible. You're trying to change your way of receiving, processing and reacting to information. A mindset that has been a part of you ever since you could reason. You've already taken the first step by acknowledging that your inner voice is part of you and that it clamors for your attention. Your inner child - the one screaming «me, me, me» - is afraid you'll leave him behind.

Will you let a child boss you around, or will you take responsibility for your thoughts and actions? I already know what your answer will be, so I've prepared the below tips to help you on your way.

1. Acknowledge your thoughts

Before you can make the most of the power of positive thinking, first you need to learn to identify your negative thoughts by paying closer attention to what's going on in your head. Over 60,000 thoughts pass through a person's head every day; most are recurrent, so we don't even notice them. As such, you have to actively find them. The negative thoughts generated by your inner voice tend to belong to one of the following categories:

- **Self-blaming**: Blaming yourself for things outside your control.

- **Fortune-telling error**: Drawing hasty conclusions about something that hasn't happened yet. «Tomorrow at the meeting I'm going to fall apart.»

- **Mind-reading**: Thinking you know what other people are thinking. «I bet they're thinking what a mess I am.»

- **Catastrophic thinking**: Exaggerating dangers and belittling your resources to face them. «If I fail this exam, I won't be able to carry on with the course.»

- **Selective attention**: Like putting on a pair of sunglasses and seeing the world through a dark lens, taking some details out of context and ignoring others, and generally interpreting things in a certain way. «My neighbor didn't say hi to me today - he's so rude.»

- **Dichotomous thinking**: Black or white with no grey areas. «I'm totally useless.»

- **Discrediting the positive**: Normalizing or minimizing good things without assigning them their true value. «What I've achieved isn't that amazing, it was pretty easy.»

- **Labeling**: Judging something based on very specific criteria. «I didn't tell them what I thought - that makes me a coward.»

- **Emotional reasoning**: Thinking that what you feel is a reality. «I feel like a misfit in class, so I must be socially inept.»

2. Reexamine the facts

What's the worst that could happen? Our thoughts are our perception of reality; however, that perception is often distorted. Our inner voice can negatively impact on our view of things. Try taking another look at the facts, objectively and with a fresh pair of eyes.

If your inner voice is telling you, you won't get that job, analyze the facts again. Why won't you get it? Don't you meet the requirements? Can't you answer the interview questions? Grab a sheet of paper, draw a line down the middle and note down the reasons for and against this negative thought. What about now? Was the negative thought correct? Every time doubt arises, get your confidence back by analyzing the facts objectively.

3. Move on

Life is not a bed of roses. You will have bad days and you will make mistakes. Constantly dwelling on them will only give your inner critic more ammunition to attack you with. Think about the event that's worrying you, and reflect on what went wrong - but bear in mind that no matter how much you go over it in your mind, you can't change what happened. All that will do is make you feel worse.

The trick to stopping this vicious cycle is to find an activity to distract you. Don't try to stop thinking about what happened, because that will just keep it at the forefront and make it difficult to move on. I suggest going out for a walk, starting a new task, meditating or picking up an old hobby again.

4. Balance acceptance and growth

Positive thinking requires you to acknowledge both your strengths and your weaknesses. However, there is a difference between accepting your flaws and giving in to them. You need to understand that you are a work in progress; recognizing your weaknesses is the first step toward a new you. As living beings, we need to keep growing and evolving - and with growth comes improvement.

5. Try using kinder words

Your thinking is affected by the kinds of words you think about and say. These words - whether directed at yourself or at others - influence your state of mind. In a conversation, your words can also affect the way people respond to you.

First, you should acknowledge the negative words in your vocabulary before you try to get rid of them. Are you terrified about that test? Or are you really just nervous? Are you pissed at Robert, or just annoyed? Note that the former words are more negative and emotionally intense.

I recommend that you make a list of the negative words that you use most often every day. Then, next to them, write a positive - or less negative - alternative. The next step is to try to introduce these new alternatives into your vocabulary. It may be hard at first, but the more you practice, the more your mindset will change and you will start to do it without even thinking.

6. Smile more

Try to see the funny side of things. Studies have shown that smiling makes you feel more positive. Genuine smiles are the most effective at this, but even a fake smile helps, as your brain can't distinguish between them so it will release endorphins just the same.

7. Surround yourself with positive people

The people around you affect your mindset; their general attitudes to life infect you. If you surround yourself with people who set goals, you will become more ambitious. In the same way, the company of negative people will increase your stress levels.

8. Persevere

At the start, you may feel you aren't making much progress. Even once you've replaced your insecurities with more productive, positive thoughts, life will continue to test you. If you truly want to begin to lead a positive life, you must never give up. Commit to taking action every single day. Create a daily ritual, have a mantra, meditate...anything that helps keep you focused. Your inner voice has been running free for years; it will take time to tame it.

9. Move forward

Your inner critic isn't just going to disappear. Nor should you want it to; you need it, to keep your feet on the ground. But, like a small child who is afraid of all change and hates the unknown, you can't let it get away with everything. You need to be the adult and take the helm.

When you understand the role of your inner voice in your negative emotions, you can find a balance between listening to it and controlling it. When you manage that, you'll become more confident and assertive, and life will make more sense and feel more rewarding.

Chapter summary

Negativity is a toxic seed, and if you allow it to grow, it can contaminate every aspect of your life. To stop negativity from controlling you and destroying everything, you need to start thinking positive. To think positive, first you must recognize your negative thoughts, reexamine the facts objectively, balance acceptance and growth, speak with kinder words, smile more, surround yourself with positive people, and - above all - persevere.

Set clear and realistic goals

«Make your vision so clear that your fears become irrelevant.»

— Anonymous

Goals give us meaning and direction, and our confidence naturally flows when we know where we are going. If you don't set goals, you will be depriving yourself of one of your greatest sources of self-confidence.

Without goals, you become an easy target for failure. Your skills will be weakened if you don't use them in a consistent, focused way; as a result, you'll lose faith in your ability to make things happen.

It's clear that goals are fundamental for self-confidence. However, most people don't know how to set goals in the right way: clear, realistic aims that give us the motivation and belief we need to break through any barrier and take a leap toward the best version of ourselves.

Imagine it's January 1st. Last year didn't go exactly how you'd hoped, so you decide to make a list of resolutions so that the next twelve months really do go exactly how you want. But before February even rolls around, your new «goals» have fallen by the wayside. Sound familiar? You'd be surprised how many people, just like you, make their New Year's resolutions full of hope - and how many, just like you, make exactly the same list year after year, because a few weeks later (maybe even a few days) they threw in the towel.

Statistics suggest that only 9% of people manage to keep their New Year's resolutions. Around 25% don't make it past the first week, 42% don't get to the fifth week, and 80% have given up by week eight. And yet every year, we prepare our «new» list of resolutions.

Many of us were never taught how to set goals in the right way. And without them, it's really hard to achieve success in a hypercompetitive society like the one we live in. It took me too long to realize this. For years, I didn't know how to set goals - or rather, I didn't know how to set them right.

Many of us know the importance of establishing aims, but few of us were taught how to do it as young children. That's why we keep making resolutions every New Year's and then abandoning them a couple of weeks later. The problem lies in the fact that a resolution is not exactly a goal. A resolution is more general and abstract, whereas a goal is much more specific.

For example, if your idea is to get fit this year, your goal could be to go to the gym a few times a week. As you can see, the goal is much clearer and more defined.

When you learn how to set clear, realistic goals, you'll form part of that 9% who manage to maintain and achieve their resolutions. I myself - like so many other people - would write the same resolutions on my New Year's list for over five years, until I finally learned to set SMART objectives.

The SMART focus for clear, realistic aims

SMART is a methodology for setting attainable goals. The model divides an aim into various guidelines, forming an acronym whereby each letter corresponds to an essential aspect of setting SMART objectives.

1. Specific

When you are setting a SMART objective, it can't be ambiguous. It's easier to stay motivated and reach a goal when it is clearly defined.

A SMART objective answers the following questions: What? How? Where? With whom?

The more information you put in, the easier it will be to achieve your goal. This will also enable you to see if you have everything you need, or if you should seek out additional resources.

2. Measurable

If you don't measure the progress of an objective, you'll never know how close you are to achieving it. That's why a SMART objective needs to be easily measurable and quantifiable.

A measurable objective answers the question: «How much?»

There is no use in simply saying «I want to make more money». A better objective would be: «I want to increase my monthly income by $500 by the end of the year.» But this type of approach can feel frustrating when the goal seems far away. Sometimes, it's easier to measure action rather than results. For example, if the necessary actions include working or studying for an extra hour each day, focus on measuring that time. I personally prefer this approach, because it allows for a more relaxed, gratifying and continual assessment.

3. Achievable

If you want to sprint 100 meters in less than ten seconds, but you're not Usain Bolt nor are you athletically-minded, you're setting yourself an unachievable goal. You're better off letting it go.

A SMART objective answers the questions: How do I do it? Can I do it? Is it realistic?

Undertaking a prior analysis and being realistic will help you to avoid unnecessary disappointment which can damage your self-confidence. As human beings, we sometimes ask too much of ourselves. It's good to get out of your comfort zone, but use your common sense.

4. Relevant

If you want something that badly, go get it.

A few years ago, nobody would have believed that Donald Trump would become the leader of the free world. A lot of people just laughed at him...until the election results were announced. Humans have achieved impossible feats and unimaginable results by having something deep within their hearts driving them to accomplish it. No one knows what they are capable of until they do it.

In order to achieve this determination and enthusiasm, you need to figure out if the goal is relevant to you at this specific point in your life.

A SMART objective answers the questions: Why? What for?

It's not enough to ask yourself: «Do I want to do this?». You may want something simply because it's what's «right» or «what people do». Instead, ask yourself: «Why do I want to do this?» Knowing the reason why will give you the motivation and discipline you need to overcome your lack of confidence and give you the ability to move mountains.

5. Time-bound

Deadlines give the things we do a sense of urgency and significance. I have realized I work more efficiently and committedly when I have a clearly defined deadline. The kind of beginning-and-end structure that a time frame gives you will create the basis for measuring your success. For example, there is a big difference between saying you want to learn a new skill by September versus just «at some point».

A SMART objective answers the question: When?

To master the SMART methodology, you need to get into the habit of always using it when setting your goals. I promise you that it's a tool with the power to change your life from the first day that you begin using it. But remember - this system will «only» help you to set the right kinds of goals. It's up to you to put them into practice!

Specific   Measurable   Achievable   Relevant   Time-bound

Four simple tips for drawing up SMART objectives

1. Prepare your action plan

Your objective is simply your final destination, your goal. You will need a plan if you want to get there. Many people focus so hard on the result that they neglect the necessary steps to reach it. To avoid making this mistake, you need to draw up a detailed action plan. A meticulous plan in writing will give you clear aims and a reference point by which to measure your progress. You can note down and document your accomplishments as well as any deviations from your initial plan. Smartphone apps can help you in this process, significantly cutting down on the time it will take you to record and measure your activities.

2. Be flexible

Just like the SMART methodology itself, I have always been of the opinion that everything should be measured and assessed. There is a saying: if you can't measure it, you can't improve on it. But this doesn't mean we should be seeking perfection in everything we do - quite the opposite. Understanding that your plan is susceptible to improvement will enable you to make changes when necessary.

When you get used to measuring your progress, you will be able to see at a glance what's working and what isn't, enabling you to adjust some objectives and add others.

3. Take responsibility

Both your actions and your lack of action must have consequences. It's important that you take responsibility. Reward yourself for doing a good job and punish yourself (within reason) when you don't fulfil your basic aims.

This carrot-and-stick system is one of the oldest and most effective systems in human civilization. Our parents and teachers used it on us when we were children, and it still works perfectly well now that we are adults. So, don't forget to reward yourself when you complete the actions you had set out for yourself, and deprive yourself of something when you don't do it. It's a little difficult, since you are your own judge, jury and executioner, so you might feel tempted to cheat. But you can always enlist someone's help to remain accountable.

4. Ask for help

We all need someone to support us. It doesn't matter if that someone is a paid professional, or a friend we can count on as an unbiased party. All you need is to find the right person - or group of people - to talk to and to support you.

Chapter summary

Setting objectives is very important, since they can send your self-esteem and confidence sky-high. It's easy to do, but setting the right objectives - the ones that can actually help you break through any barrier - requires a system. SMART is a method that will enable you to set suitable goals by following five simple guidelines based on its acronym: Specific, Measurable, Achievable, Relevant and Time-bound. Once you've set your SMART objectives, you will need: a good action plan, to be flexible and make any necessary changes, to take responsibility - by rewarding or punishing yourself as you move through the tasks you've set yourself - and to ask for help when your objective requires it.

STEP 5

....

Lean on healthy relationships

«A healthy relationship will never require you to sacrifice your friends, your dreams or your dignity.»

— Mandy Hale

Healthy relationships are formed between two or more people who love and respect each other deeply, with positive, two-way communication. They lean on and encourage one another, trust each other and - at the same time - exist as free and independent beings.

We can have healthy relationships with anyone. It might be your parents, friends, teachers, or the waiter at your favorite diner... We relate to other people every day, and life is much easier when our interactions with those people occur in the context of a healthy relationship. The benefits of these kinds of relationships are countless. Now, the problem is that not all of our relationships may be healthy.

Many people are stuck in unhealthy relationships with poor communication, unable to freely express themselves. These relationships may turn toxic and end up ruining us, destroying our self-esteem and self-confidence. Let me share a story that perfectly demonstrates the huge impact that a toxic - or at least, unhealthy - relationship can have on our lives.

During a placement for the master's in Business Management that I did when I was 29, I met Emma, a girl a few years younger than me who was doing a placement at the same company. From the moment I met her, I realized Emma barely spoke to our colleagues. She scarcely ever said anything more than «good morning», and she always avoided situations where she might have to talk to people. Fortunately, we managed to bond over our love of series and I gradually gained her trust as we became friends.

One day, Emma told me that her parents had divorced when she was seven. Her father had met another woman and started a new family, and she had stayed with her mother. At first, she saw her dad every weekend, but over the years the visits dwindled until she hardly saw him. Sadly, things were far from perfect with her mom, either; after the divorce, she had thrown herself into her career, so they spent little time together and Emma was usually either home alone or at a neighbor's house.

Her parents' total lack of participation in her childhood and adolescence had profoundly affected her self-confidence - perhaps because she felt that it had all been her fault - and it negatively impacted on all her other relationships.

During her high school years, Emma got into several unhealthy romantic relationships and ended up being known as the «sure thing», who would do anything to please others.

It may seem that these kinds of relationships are just «high school drama» that most people go through and get over, but it went deeper than that for Emma. The relationships that she got into during this time only served to aggravate her problem and further undermine her already fragile self-esteem.

At college, the few «friends» she had didn't help at all; some either took advantage or were embarrassed of her in equal amounts, and some were in a similar situation themselves. So, just like in high school, to avoid feeling alone, Emma spent most of her time in selfish, superficial relationships where she had to beg for attention from toxic guys who mistreated her psychologically, and sometimes even physically.

It wasn't until she finished college - shortly before starting the master's course on which I met her - that she realized that something wasn't right. «I realized that I had wasted most of my years at college on people who, at best, didn't care about me at all.»

As a result of accepting this small part of her reality, she lost interest in people in general and decided to switch off from the world. After college and until we met, Emma had become a lone wolf. She mistrusted anyone who tried to get close to her, and avoided any kind of interaction because she believed she had nothing to offer. She admitted to me: «At this point, I don't even feel in charge of my life. I just get up and go to work. I have no future plans. I don't think my goals are valid or that I deserve them.»

Luckily for Emma, at that time I was already well-versed in the world of personal development, and although I wasn't the right person to help her (it's best for your therapist or life coach not to be a friend of yours), I was able to recommend a good professional. They began sessions together, and he helped her to turn her life around in just a few short months, gaining self-confidence and getting back the feeling of being in control over her life. Nowadays, Emma enjoys healthy friendships, she's married to a great guy, and they have plans and goals both together and as individuals, which fills their lives with sense and meaning.

Emma's story is just one example of how toxic, unhealthy relationships can damage your confidence and self-esteem, and the devastating effects that this can have long-term. I'm sure you're perfectly capable of identifying those people around you who continually undermine your confidence and cause you to doubt in your own abilities with their sarcastic or disparaging comments. It doesn't matter who they are or what relation they are to you; **get them out of your life**.

Ask yourself: Does this person or relationship help me to be the best version of myself? Do they bring balance to my life, support me and encourage me to achieve my aims?

If the answer is no, why are you still in that relationship? Why are you still dedicating your time to that person? What good are your friends, family, colleagues or partners to you if they don't bring anything good into your life?

If you want to develop self-confidence of steel, **you have to get rid of the people who are not helping you grow.**

Chapter summary

Fostering healthy relationships is one of the bases for increasing your self-confidence. The benefits of this kind of relationship include a reduction in stress, a general improvement to your mood, increased life expectancy, a renewed sense of purpose and the ability to pursue your goals without fear. We all deserve to be surrounded by people who love and respect us, deeply and sincerely. We must not allow toxic people or relationships to be in our lives.

STEP 6

Be ready for setbacks; divide and conquer your problems

«Success consists of going from failure to failure without loss of enthusiasm.»

— Winston Churchill

In science fiction movies, it usually takes several attempts before scientists manage to develop a prototype that works (be it a machine, a code, a cure for zombies...). I know movies exaggerate, but they're not wrong on this: it might take ten, hundred or a thousand tries before the protagonist finally gets it right. It's inevitable that you will fail on the path to success. So, be aware that setbacks will occur. Failure can present itself in the form of small mistakes or huge screw-ups with far-reaching consequences. This is the price of getting into action, of giving it a try, of leaving your comfort zone.

The high likelihood of these setbacks occurring makes it surprising that so many people fail to prepare for them. When you don't prepare for something, you are allowing your instincts to lead you. This is dangerous because the way in which you manage and react to failure affects your chances of success. Small mistakes - not to mention major difficulties - can be a great blow to your self-confidence, particularly if you are already unsure of yourself. But with the right preparation, you can reduce the impact of any setbacks.

Preparing for failure means anticipating it. This doesn't mean that you actually want it to happen, of course. What you're trying to do here is reduce its impact by creating realistic expectations and developing contingency plans to help you manage any obstacles. Let's use the analogy of riding a motorbike. Riders use protective equipment, like helmets and jackets. Wearing them doesn't mean the rider wants to get in an accident; they are merely trying to reduce the risks if one does happen. If you are properly prepared, you can conquer failure and improve your chances of success.

Why you should stop being afraid of failure, and how to turn setbacks into opportunities

1. Problems means opportunities

Don't let your fear of failure stop you from doing what you need to do to triumph. Setbacks mean that you are moving forward, which means success is on the horizon. We as people are afraid of making mistakes because we see them as a reflection on our skills and personalities. But people who achieve success after numerous failures are proof that mistakes come from our actions, not from us as people.

Letting your results define you is a sign that you are putting all your hopes into the actions that will get you those results. It's an all-or-nothing mentality. But we both know that this doesn't work in reality. You need to see each of your actions for what it is: one of many possible tries or experiments. If the experiment pays off, then great! If it doesn't...try it another way. But always try to make sure the next experiment is better than the last. Look at the strengths and weaknesses of your past attempts in order to modify, innovate and improve.

We tend to underestimate these little adjustments. The only way to see their potential is to take further action, to try again, to make more mistakes and to suffer further setbacks. Athletes have to train harder, fall more times, take on more opponents. Experience is the only way to keep getting better. So don't be afraid of setbacks - learn from them, and get better, stronger, and smarter.

2. Learn and improve

It's easy to manage and overcome small mistakes. But some setbacks are more serious and traumatic. They may change who you are and turn you into a completely different person. A therapist would say that such a person has allowed failure to define them.

Look at mistakes as lessons: lessons that bring you valuable knowledge. Follow scientists' example - all their discoveries and innovations came about after multiple failed attempts. If you're an entrepreneur and you find yourself picking yourself up from your twenty-sixth failed attempt at developing the hoverboard from Back to the Future, don't say: «I failed twenty-six times». Instead, say: «I found twenty-six ways that don't work!».

A person who wants to grow can't allow themselves the luxury of a fear of failure. Our entire civilization was built by failing, learning, and improving. Don't expect to go from zero to a hundred in a smooth, uninterrupted trajectory. Some people may be lucky enough not to have faced difficulties, setbacks or disappointment. But remember: they are the exception, not the rule. Even people like Steve Jobs, Winston Churchill and Alexander the Great had their problems. If you want to change your life and achieve greatness, I'm afraid failure is part of the package. The question is, will you let it sink you, or will you use it to your advantage?

3. Failure is the best teacher

The truth is that we tend not to talk about failure - either the failures of famous people in history, or those of people closer to us. Maybe we focus on success stories because it's nicer to listen to than hearing how things went wrong. Well, this is a mistake - there's a lot more to learn from failure than there is from success.

In any case, success can make us arrogant and big-headed. How many child stars went off the rails before they were twenty-five? Compare them with actors who didn't get their big break until they were in their late twenties or early thirties. These stars tend to be more mature, motivated and humble. Years of rejection and hard work can have this positive effect on people.

Success is the ultimate goal, but you will have to deal with obstacles along the way. Michael Jordan said: «I've failed over and over and over again in my life. And that is why I succeed.» People who have experienced life's problems are less likely to be complacent. Getting out of your comfort zone carries the risk of failure - but courageous people see setbacks as opportunities for success.

4. Grow from your mistakes

Up till now, I've only talked about the advantages of setbacks - it would be highly irresponsible of me not to admit that not all mistakes or setbacks are equal. Yes, you can learn from your mistakes - but not all of them will be worth it. Remember that preparing for setbacks also helps reduce the risk of failure.

Don't jump into anything with your eyes closed. You need to calculate the risk of every adventure you embark on. Be as responsible with your setbacks as you are with your aims. And remember that mistakes are failures of actions, not of the people making them. Focus on your actions, pay close attention, and learn from them.

5. Change your mindset

What is failure if not success in disguise? Understanding this will help to mitigate your fear of failure. When we look at others' successes from afar, it's easy to ignore all the failures they had to go through. Similarly, other people may have the same view of your own victories and think they simply fell into your lap.

Setbacks are part of the path to success, so when one crops up, take it as a sign that you are still on that path, so you can't have failed yet. All you have done is discover a route that didn't work. The only logical option is to find a new route that will get you closer to your destination. If you can view setbacks as opportunities to try new and exciting adventures, you'll be one step closer to success.

6. Learn from other people

We humans have been battling the same problems for so long that you can be sure that someone, somewhere, has faced the same obstacle you are facing right now. Learn from them. We live in the information era - I bet you can find dozens of books and hundreds of interesting articles with just a quick Google. Set some time aside to read biographies of famous people, and take note of both their successes and their failures.

Every time you experience a major setback and you feel like you can't keep going, go back to those books. Let the stories of your idols inspire and motivate you. You can also ask for advice from the people around you - but remember that many people will try to dissuade you from taking any kind of risk. Conformism and fear of failure will make you a mediocre person; the ability to take (controlled) risks will see you rise above the rest.

Divide and conquer

Ancient military strategies have now infiltrated several aspects of our lives. Top executives read «The Art of War» at bedtime, politicians use Machiavellian tactics and entrepreneurs apply the teachings of Alexander the Great. «Divide and conquer» is one of the oldest strategies in existence. Nowadays, we can find it in every sector, from athletic academies to computer manufacturing.

This strategy became popular because it is very useful when it comes to managing demanding and complex tasks: ones that seem insurmountable all in one go. Let's imagine you have a task to perform that feels so huge and challenging that you are paralyzed, feeling incapable of carrying it out. All you have to do is break down this large task into several smaller, more manageable sub-tasks. That way, you can complete them one by one.

Here's an example of how this tactic works.

Imagine you are nervous because you have to attend a work event you really don't want to go to. The first step is to figure out the minimum acceptable time you really have to stay at the event before you can leave. Let's say you decide that you can leave after forty-five minutes. Now, all you have to do is «survive» for as long as that :)

Write up a list of the things you'll need to do during those forty-five minutes. Do you need to mingle with your colleagues, gain X number of new contacts, discuss a project with a coworker, or spend a few minutes kissing your boss's ass? Assign an order and a length of time to each of these tasks, and once you're at the event, complete them one by one before moving on to the next. You can even set alarms if you want - but I guarantee that once you start, you'll forget all about the time as you move through the items on your list.

«Divide and conquer» works for work, weight loss, personal development and much more. You will already be using it without realizing. All you have to do now is use it more often and in a more conscious way.

Chapter summary

Life isn't perfect; you can expect setbacks, failures and disappointments. This doesn't mean you should be negative - it means you should be prepared for any outcome. First, remind yourself that more setbacks equal more opportunities. This will change your mindset and help you to learn from your mistakes and grow from your failures. So don't get disheartened if you fall. Don't let failure leave its mark on your confidence. On the contrary: consider it an opportunity to get better and to keep moving toward the best version of yourself.

STEP 7

Improve your skills and develop your competence

«Continuous learning is the minimum requirement for success in any field.»
— Denis Waitley

Being competent makes you feel more confident. Competent people hold their heads high wherever they go. There is no greater feeling than knowing you can do what others can't, and do it well. Competence will provide a huge boost to your self-confidence.

Competence should be a process of continuous improvement. The moment you stop is the moment you start to get rusty. There is always something you can improve on. So, look at your quest for competence as a journey that doesn't end until you die.

Don't think you've already reached your full potential just because you're above average or doing better than those around you. Growth must be followed by more growth. Apply this philosophy to every area of your life. Always strive to improve all your skills and seek to grow within yourself, your career, and your relationships with others.

Sportspeople don't stop training when they're doing well. Usually, they actually increase the intensity of their workouts when they're doing well, since they have people and goals that motivate them to keep going. These could be rivals, coaches, or simply glory.

You may not have the luxury of your own personal trainer to motivate you to keep moving forward. In this case, just like for most of us mere mortals, the responsibility falls to you. Figure out what areas interest you most, and develop your skills to become more competent. If you train in these fields, you will become more efficient, make fewer mistakes, and achieve more success, which will cause your confidence to skyrocket.

Confidence, or the lack of it, is a personal matter. Your intrapersonal relationship has more of an impact on your confidence than your interpersonal relationships. It's up to you whether you are your own best friend or your own worst enemy. If you choose to be the former, then prioritize your personal development.

Assess the effects that your flaws and virtues have on your aims. Then, develop the skills you need to achieve said aims. Personal development is about maturing and maximizing your potential in order to lead a fuller life. It's like your own personal evolution. You will continue to develop your skills and broaden your knowledge for the rest of your life. Education doesn't end with school. Remember: you don't need a teacher in order to keep learning, although a good mentor is always handy.

The first step will be to think carefully about what knowledge you want to acquire. Knowledge takes up no space, and your brain has an almost unlimited capacity for learning - unfortunately, your time *is* limited. So, choose carefully which skills hold the greatest potential - those that will most help you to grow both personally and professionally - and focus on them. It's called self-development because it is up to you to identify and develop the skills that are important to you and to your life success.

Essential skills you should strive to improve

1. Leadership

If you want people to follow you, you must learn to lead. We remember great leaders for their ability to get others to share their objectives and how they motivate the people around them. Followers are a reflection of their leader.

2. Social skills

Also known as interpersonal skills. We are all aware of the importance of verbal and non-verbal communication and master these to a greater or lesser extent. Improving your social skills will make it easier for those around you to understand and relate to you.

3. Communication

You are a good communicator if the way you speak, listen and write is clear, efficient and concise. You have certain ideas and feelings, and the person you are communicating with has others. Unless you're a mind-reader, communication is the only way to transmit and receive information between two or more individuals. A lack of communicative skills has started wars, caused deaths and generated millions of conflicts throughout human history - so it's not a skill you want to underestimate or assume you have already mastered. Your chances of success will increase if you learn to speak clearly and to use the right tone for each occasion.

4. Problem-solving

The difference between people who triumph and people who fail usually lies in their ability to solve problems. The only way to avoid problems entirely is not to get out of bed in the morning. And given that this is not an option, you have to learn to face problems. Objectively assessing them and coming up with solutions that work is one of the skills that will most help you to prosper in life.

5. Organization

We humans - at least most of us - like order and predictability. I don't know about you, but chaos makes me uncomfortable and therefore less productive. Learning to organize, plan and schedule will make your life simpler and more rewarding.

6. Integrity

Warren Buffet said: «Look for three things in a person: intelligence, energy and integrity. If they don't have the last one, don't even bother with the first two.» Integrity is what will make people trust you. It's the quality that makes you tell the truth and do the right thing. People around you will know that your «yes» means «yes», and your «no», «no».

7. Adaptability

Life will throw you a curveball from time to time. When it seems that nothing could surprise you, it will turn out the universe has something up its sleeve. Learn to navigate new and unknown situations. Stay calm and adapt quickly.

How to develop these skills

Once you have identified what skills are important for you (I'm sure you can think of lots more that aren't on my list), the next step is to develop them.

1. Set clear objectives

I advise you to go back over the chapter on goal setting. Apply the SMART method to create your self-development objectives. When you're trying to improve several skills at once, it's best to approach them one by one. Remember: divide and conquer.

2. Read

Read, watch educational videos and do online courses. Knowledge is power, as they say. Read around your goals and acquire the necessary knowledge for achieving them. However, don't limit your reading solely to concrete objectives. Reading can also help you to expand your vocabulary, stimulate your mind and discover new things. In short, read as much as you can - both for work and for pleasure.

3. Write

Despite what you may think, keeping a diary isn't just for teenagers. It's just about noting down ideas and thoughts so that you don't forget them. Write about your aims, your battles, your achievements, your strengths and your insecurities. I have a physical diary as well as several apps so that I can keep a record of these kinds of ideas. I use the diary for doing some leisurely writing when I sit down for a coffee, for example, and the apps for jotting down ideas that come to me when I'm on the go.

4. Find a mentor

You need people to admire and trust. Having a figure in your life who has already traveled the path you're on now will accelerate your growth exponentially. If you don't have anyone like this in your life and you can't afford to hire a professional, I recommend that you find your «guru» in books or online and study them carefully. You can read their books, watch their videos or do their (free) courses.

5. Ask for feedback

It's important that you don't ignore this part. Make an extra effort to find people who can offer you honest, constructive criticism of your personal and professional life. Ask your friends, family, coworkers and superiors for their opinions. Simply asking them what they think of you is too abstract to get you a good answer. Instead, ask them what they think of specific behavior or projects. That will get you a much more precise answer that you can work on in order to improve.

People very close to you may give you very biased, partial opinions. You may prefer to hear the opinions of people from outside your inner circle, as they have not yet formed an opinion of you and therefore have no reason to dress up their comments for fear of hurting your feelings.

Chapter summary

Competence is a potent source of confidence. Sometimes, it's not enough to know how to do something - you need to know you can do it better than other people. In order to develop your competence, you must first work on various aspects of yourself, like your social, organizational or leadership skills. You will find it helpful to set some clear goals, keep a record of your ideas and thoughts, find a mentor and ask for opinions both from people close to you and people who aren't.

Walk before you can run

«Big things have small beginnings.»
— T. E. Lawrence

The phrase «go big or go home» is a fallacy. It only works in very specific situations, and in any case, the chances of failing are so elevated that most smart people elect not to take this «quick» route, as they understand the benefits of a slow, methodical approach. I call the big-steps approach a high-risk one, and small steps low-risk. The former requires too many resources - which so many of us don't have - to be a valid, potentially successful option.

I know, you strive for great things - so do I. We don't want to fly coach when we can travel up front. And this translates into every aspect of our lives; our eye is often caught by big, shiny things. But what we must not forget is that those big things didn't grow on trees. Great achievements always had humble beginnings. Remember that Apple, Facebook and Microsoft started in garages.

Think about the most enduring companies or ideas you know, and you'll notice a trend. They all began from something small. So, if you want to make lasting changes in your life, take note. Confidence - or a lack of it - is a habit. It's something rooted in your subconscious and the only way to achieve solid change at this level is with slow, constant focus. Slow beginnings have the advantage of being easier to get going and keep under control. They are also easier to build and maintain. Don't get me wrong - dream big, want big things, but start small.

1. Be prepared

Every adventure worth going on warrants proper preparation. Even then, you have to understand you will never be completely ready. Be careful not to let your preparation turn into an excuse to procrastinate. Set a time limit for the preparation stage, and once it's passed, get started! Preparation is the first step to achieving any change you want, but it's a step that must be carried out quickly and efficiently.

2. Start with baby steps

Don't underestimate the power of simplicity. Your first steps should be simple and accessible. Some people believe you should tackle the big things first, and leave the finer details for later. This is not an approach I recommend if you want to gain confidence. It only works for a small percentage of people - even if they are a vocal minority. Confidence, like other important traits, is like a little seed; you have to nourish it and allow it to grow before it can put down roots. For example, if you've set yourself the aim of working out five hours a week, you're more likely to achieve (and maintain) this if you spread those five hours out over several days rather than trying to do it all in one day.

3. Stay motivated and disciplined

You need motivation to get started, and discipline to keep going. This shouldn't be too hard if you believe that your objectives are achievable. That's why it's so important to start with aims that are not overwhelming. Of course, you'll have to boost your self-motivation as things get a little more difficult and obstacles appear, but for now, just focus on taking those first steps. Let your accomplishment of those first, smaller aims help to motivate you and encourage you to keep moving forward.

4. Start little by little before seeking bigger challenges

The aim of starting small-scale is to gain experience and familiarize yourself with the change. However, growth stops when that familiarity reaches a certain point. At that point, you stop growing and improving. Confidence is like a child; you have to keep feeding it bigger and bigger challenges or it will plateau and may even regress. I would tell you that you should increase the difficulty of the task every few steps, but this would require a carefully measured plan to determine when you are ready to move up to the next level. Instead, a rule that works really well is: «do more than you did last week». So start with small steps, but plan to take it further.

5. Be consistent

Consistency generates experience, confidence and drive. The last of these is the most important.

If you feed something, it becomes bigger and stronger. Constantly taking action will feed your confidence and create drive. It's a cycle that you break every time you skip or postpone a step - so do what you have to, even when you don't feel like it. This is where responsibility and discipline play an important role. They will help you create a reward/punishment system like the one we talked about in step 4.

Consistency also makes you hungry for success. Starting with baby steps increases your chances of this success. These small wins will stoke your appetite, which will make you try harder and be better prepared to take the leap.

Chapter summary

Small actions add up to big results. When you take baby steps, you give yourself more wiggle room to make mistakes and learn from them. In addition, small steps will enable you to celebrate small wins, which will feed your confidence and create the drive you need to take on bigger challenges. If you elect to make radical changes all in one go, you will expend more resources and find it harder to bounce back from failure, which will end up undermining your confidence.

STEP 9

Learn to expect - and deal with - negative criticism

«There is only one way to avoid criticism: do nothing, say nothing, and be nothing.»

— Aristóteles

If you learn how to use criticism - constructive or otherwise - in your favor, not only will it not damage your self-confidence, it will actually increase it.

I decided to leave this step till last for two reasons: firstly, because for me, it is the most potent strategy if you know how to use it correctly, and secondly, because it just might be the least obvious one.

LIBERATE YOURSELF: Whatever you do, there will always be people to criticize you, so do whatever you want.

Kathy, my girlfriend, is an amazing woman in every single respect: she's cheerful, smart, athletic, entrepreneurial, ... I could go on, since I have the good habit of noting down in a little book every good thing I discover about her since the day we met - something I recommend you do, too.

Unfortunately, she is also the older of two sisters in a family which - while I am sure they love her very much - decided to make her a target for their criticism. It doesn't matter what she does, her sister and mother are always reproaching her and looking down their noses at her. If she studies, she should work and stop being «silly»; if she works, she should study and aim higher. If she helps her family out financially, she's showing off; if she doesn't, she's selfish. If she begins a project, she's living in la la land; if she doesn't, she should start up a bar (what?!). And so on and so forth, her whole life.

When I met her, Kathy was suffering from frequent anxiety attacks - more or less every time there was a family gathering. Whenever they got together, her mother and sister would go in all guns blazing, trying hard to undermine her confidence and her lust for life.

Although I work professionally with clients in very similar situations, when it came to my partner, it was complicated for me to get involved. This was partly because advice from a partner (or close friend) tends to be taken less seriously and have less of an impact than advice from a «paid» professional, and partly because it could have created family conflict that would end up pushing us apart. Have you ever heard that blood is thicker than water? Well, that was the problem.

Eventually, I could no longer tolerate the unfairness of the situation and how it was affecting Kathy, and I decided to act in the most subtle way I could think of. The day after one of those family gatherings, after Kathy came home crying and feeling worthless, I sent an «innocent» comic to her cellphone:

Obviously, the comic didn't resolve the problem by itself - but it did make Kathy smile and realize how ridiculous the situation was and that she could totally relate. It was a great starting point for talking about it all - a conversation Kathy herself started when she got home from work that evening.

Kathy realized that her anxiety was mainly occurring because, ever since she could remember, every step she took in life had been on eggshells, afraid of what her mother and sister would say. She would end up taking the paths she thought they would most approve of. Sadly, her decisions never managed to meet their standards, and she just became more and more unhappy.

But when she realized that, for whatever reason, she had lost the battle before it had even begun - since she would never be able to please the two people she loved most in the world - she felt liberated. It's not that she didn't care any more about their approval; she simply no longer needed it.

From then on, Kathy began to make decisions and choose her path based solely on what she thought was best. On the one hand, she had enough confidence to know what she wanted without having to consult with anybody else, and on the other, she knew that she could not, and should not have to, please everyone.

EMPOWER YOURSELF: Learn to view criticism from another perspective.

It is hugely liberating to realize that regardless of what you do, you will never please everyone at once - but there's a big difference between feeling liberated from criticism and feeling empowered *by* criticism.

Although I'm lucky enough to have parents who have always supported me through all my projects and decisions, I have still - like my girlfriend - had to deal with unending, brutal criticism from other family members.

For many years, this criticism kept me conditioned and frustrated. Nothing I could do or say could win those people's approval. I remember thinking: «someday, they'll realize my worth», «maybe if I achieve this or that, they'll congratulate me», «what am I doing wrong? Why don't they like me?», and so on.

It took me a long time to realize that nothing I ever did would be good enough for them. The day I figured that out (like I'm hoping you are now) I felt liberated, but it wasn't until I understood **the reason for these attacks** that I realized I had something special: something that made me unique and amazing.

What did my girlfriend and I have in common to make us the target of criticism from our loved ones? I'll give you a clue: it's what made us fall for each other within minutes of meeting for breaking (thanks, Tinder). We are both «doers»: we have ideas, aims, plans...**and we actually carry them out**.

When you are someone who not only has goals, but fights for them - and more often than not achieves them - you become an inconvenient mirror for others. People will look at you and realize that they did not persist hard enough to reach their dreams, or - worse - they never really knew what they wanted in life in the first place, until it was too late[1].

When you realize that the criticism that hurt you and your self-confidence so badly in the past was actually an indicator that you were on the right track - a track that others secretly wanted to

---

[1] If this is you, you can't afford not to read The power of goals: http://mybook.to/yourbestself1

be on themselves - then not only will criticism stop affecting you, but you will actually begin to seek it out. It will be your new indicator that you're doing things right, and that you're aiming high enough to inspire envy. Do you really think anyone is going to bother to try and undermine your confidence (be it consciously or not) with their criticism if you stay with the flock, content with mediocrity, never stepping foot outside your comfort zone?

I'll give you an example to make it clearer - an example you may even have lived through:

I'm sure you know someone who always struggled with their weight, and then one day, for no apparent reason (although believe me, there will have been a reason), they decided to start eating right and join the gym. In a few short months, they had lost a considerable amount of weight and their appearance was beginning to show how they would look at a healthy weight. Criticism? Of course not; everyone around them was happy for them and their new lifestyle, and encouraged them to keep going. As you'd expect - after all, what kind of heartless person would criticize that kind of personal improvement?

But what would happen if that person managed to maintain their new habits? Not just for a few months - which is what normally happens - but for long enough that they go from being obese to being a healthy weight, and from there to having an enviable body? Criticism? Flying all over the place: «Look, he's obsessed», «she's not getting paid to do this», «he's not enjoying his life», «who does she think she is?», «he should put down the weights and pick up a book», «she must be having an affair with that kind of weight loss», and so on. Sound familiar?

We encourage and praise our friends and loved ones to help them fight to get to where we are now; we want them to be part of our «tribe», our flock, at our level. But watch out - that's as far as it goes. For anyone unwilling to pay the price to keep growing and achieving new goals, the only way of not getting left behind and leading a life they regret is to try and stop *you* from getting ahead. For these people, criticism is one of their most powerful weapons.

Until now.

Now that you know why people criticize you in this way, not only will you be immune to their attacks - you'll actually understand that the fact they're criticizing you is a great sign. It's a sign you're on the right track. Don't let anything stop you.

Always remember this saying:

«You will never be criticized by people who are doing more than you, only by people who are doing less or doing nothing.»

Chapter summary

In life, the only way to keep yourself safe from criticism is to do absolutely nothing. Given that this is not an option, you have to learn to deal with criticism in order to stop it from destroying your confidence and limiting your potential. The first step is to understand that no matter what you do, people will criticize you. The day you accept this sad truth, you will feel liberated, and criticism will lose its power over you. Only by doing this can you open up a world of possibilities - but you can go one step further and actually utilize criticism in your favor, to motivate you and reaffirm your actions and goals. All you have to do is remember that only mediocre people who never leave their comfort zone and stick with the herd are protected from criticism. If you receive constant criticism from those around you, it's likely that you are secretly envied; people can't bear the idea that you might achieve what they couldn't, because they let their fears be bigger than their goals.

The next steps

At the start of this book, I promised I would give you the knowledge you needed to make this journey toward greater self-confidence easy, and you promised you would spring into action and allow this knowledge to become a part of you, enabling you to lead the life you always dreamed of.

Now that we've reached the end of these nine steps, all that's left for me to do is congratulate you.

In truth, your journey began the moment you decided to buy this book, and the fact you've come this far means **you've already sprung into action**.

CONGRATULATIONS!

So many people would like to improve their confidence, and envy those who seem to possess it naturally - but only a few decide to take matters into their own hands and act on it. You belong to this small proportion of courageous people, and you should feel proud.

But be careful not to rest on your laurels. You've taken a very important first step, but you have work still to do. You might have internalized some of the steps in this book already, while others may require a second reading and others still might demand more from you.

Don't worry - you don't need to put all of them into practice in one go. Choose the step you like best or that seems easiest, and focus on that until you internalize it and it comes naturally to you. You already know that when you do things little by little, the feeling of accomplishment from achieving that first step or objective will give you the confidence and motivation you need to take on the next step with energy and gusto. That next step may consist of something as simple as beginning to carry a diary around with you to write down your goals, or deciding to spend less time with people who bring you nothing (or nothing good, anyway), or making a list of the skills you have that could most improve your life.

It's up to you. Only you have the power to transform your life and turn that void you've always felt inside into an unending source of satisfaction and contentment. Don't put it off until tomorrow. Decide today what your next step will be, and get to it.

The life you want is waiting for you.

Take care!
Daniel

Many thanks from my girlfriend Kathy, our rabbit Snoopy, and me, of course ;)

Your opinion matters

As I'm an independent author, your opinion is so important to me and to future readers like you. I would be hugely grateful if you would leave me **a review on your favorite store** to tell me what you thought of my book **so that I can keep on improving it**:

- What did you like best?
- Is there anything you felt was missing
- Who would you recommend it to?
- ...

A gift just for you!

Would you like to **read my next book completely FREE?** Scan the code below and **join my readers' club!**

Great surprises await: be the first to read my new releases, listen to my audiobooks for free, get signed and dedicated copies... and much more!

www.danieljmartin.es/readersclub/

Other books by Daniel J. Martin